MW00910333

Childhoods
of the
Presidents

James
Madison

Childhoods
of the
Presidents

John Adams

George W. Bush

Bill Clinton

Ulysses S. Grant

Andrew Jackson

Thomas Jefferson

John F. Kennedy

Abraham Lincoln

James Madison

James Monroe

Ronald Reagan

Franklin D. Roosevelt

Theodore Roosevelt

Harry S. Truman

George Washington

Woodrow Wilson

James
Madison

Lisa Kozleski

Mason Crest Publishers
Philadelphia

Produced by OTTN Publishing, Stockton, New Jersey

Mason Crest Publishers
370 Reed Road
Broomall, PA 19008
www.masoncrest.com

Copyright © 2003 by Mason Crest Publishers. All rights reserved. Printed and bound in the Hashemite Kingdom of Jordan.

First printing

1 3 5 7 9 8 6 4 2

Library of Congress Cataloging-in-Publication Data

Kozleski, Lisa.
    James Madison / Lisa Kozleski.
        p.   cm.   (Childhood of the presidents)
    Summary: A biography of the fourth president of the United States, focusing on his childhood and young adulthood.
    Includes bibliographical references (p.) and index.
        ISBN 1-59084-269-3
    1. Madison, James, 1751-1836—Childhood and youth—Juvenile literature. 2. Madison, James, 1751-1836—Juvenile literature.
    3. Presidents—United States—Biography—Juvenile literature.
    [1. Madison, James, 1751-1836—Childhood and youth.
    2. Presidents.] I. Title. II. Series.
    E342.K69 2003
    973.5'1'092—dc21
    [B]   2002069246

Publisher's note: All quotations in this book come from original sources, and contain the spelling and grammatical inconsistencies of the original text.

Childhoods of the Presidents

Table of Contents

★★★★★★★★★★★★★★★★

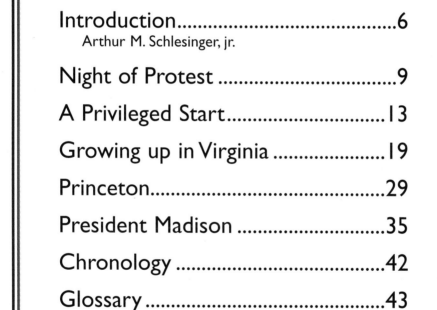

★ *Introduction* ★

Alexis de Tocqueville began his great work *Democracy in America* with a discourse on childhood. If we are to understand the prejudices, the habits and the passions that will rule a man's life, Tocqueville said, we must watch the baby in his mother's arms; we must see the first images that the world casts upon the mirror of his mind; we must hear the first words that awaken his sleeping powers of thought. "The entire man," he wrote, "is, so to speak, to be seen in the cradle of the child."

That is why these books on the childhoods of the American presidents are so much to the point. And, as our history shows, a great variety of childhoods can lead to the White House. The record confirms the ancient adage that every American boy, no matter how unpromising his beginnings, can aspire to the presidency. Soon, one hopes, the adage will be extended to include every American girl.

All our presidents thus far have been white males who, within the limits of their gender, reflect the diversity of American life. They were born in nineteen of our states; eight of the last thirteen presidents were born west of the Mississippi. Of all our presidents, Abraham Lincoln had the least promising childhood, yet he became our greatest president. Oddly enough, presidents who are children of privilege sometimes feel an obligation to reform society in order to give children of poverty a better break. And, with Lincoln the great exception, presidents who are children of poverty sometimes feel that there is no need to reform a society that has enabled them to rise from privation to the summit.

Does schooling make a difference? Harry S. Truman, the only twentieth-century president never to attend college, is generally accounted a near-great president. Actually nine— more than one fifth—of our presidents never went to college at all, including such luminaries as George Washington, Andrew Jackson and Grover Cleveland. But, Truman aside, all the non-college men held the highest office before the twentieth century, and, given the increasing complexity of life, a college education will unquestionably be a necessity in the twenty-first century.

Every reader of this book, girls included, has a right to aspire to the presidency. As you survey the childhoods of those who made it, try to figure out the qualities that brought them to the White House. I would suggest that among those qualities are ambition, determination, discipline, education— and luck.

—ARTHUR M. SCHLESINGER, JR.

American colonists protest the Stamp Act, a British tax on printed materials, by burning newspapers. In 1770 the patriotic fervor of the young James Madison was similarly awakened at a bonfire in support of a boycott of British goods.

Night of Protest

The bonfire crackled and snapped, illuminating the evening sky with the glow of its orange and red flames. A speaker stood on a low platform, holding up a piece of paper and shouting angry words. The crowd surrounding the fire roared its approval. Nearly all of the people in the crowd were young men. Most were students at the College of New Jersey in Princeton, New Jersey. The year was 1770, and the students were angry with the government of Great Britain, the country that ruled the 13 American colonies at the time.

Many people in the colonies were unhappy with the British government. After the end of the French and Indian War in 1763, the British had forced the Americans to pay new taxes. The government said that the taxes were necessary to help repay the cost of the war, which had been fought mostly on the western borders of the 13 colonies. However, the Americans argued that the taxes were unfair. The colonies were not represented in *Parliament*, the part of the English government that made the laws. If they had no say in the laws made by Parliament, colonial leaders argued, then it wasn't fair to force them to pay taxes.

England had established the colonies in the 17th and early 18th centuries. Over the years trade between the colonies and England had been profitable. The colonists sold raw materials—timber, tobacco, cotton, and other products—to merchants in England. In return, English merchants sent finished goods—books, furniture, glass windowpanes, and rolls of linen and cotton cloth—to the colonies, where they could be sold.

In 1767, the British government placed a tax on finished goods sent to the colonies. In response, merchants from the 13 colonies decided not to buy goods from England unless they were absolutely necessary. They hoped the tax would be *repealed* once the English merchants saw their sales—and profits—falling.

The letter the speaker waved from the platform at the College of New Jersey that night in 1770 was from a group of merchants in New York. The merchants were thinking about ending their **boycott** of English goods. They wanted to know how merchants in the other colonies would react if they began buying from the British again.

The reaction of the students was clear. They cheered as the speaker crumpled the letter and threw it into the bonfire. They didn't want American merchants to give in and accept the British taxes.

In the crowd of angry students that night was a young man from Virginia. He believed strongly in the American cause and was inspired by the protest at the College of New Jersey. In a few years, as Americans fought for their independence from Great Britain, he would become an important and respected American political leader. His name was James Madison.

At first glance young James Madison didn't look like much of a leader. He was small—standing just 5 feet 4 inches tall and weighing only about 100 pounds. He spoke in a soft voice. When he did discuss a subject in public, he wasn't a very inspirational speaker. Rather than try to win his audience over with impassioned speech, he preferred to use logic to make his points. He seemed destined to settle down to the life of a well-to-do Virginia landowner—like his father and grandfather—not to become a leader admired by millions of Americans.

But those who looked past James Madison's soft voice and quiet demeanor would have been impressed with his intelligence, as well as with his dedication to the ideals on which America would be founded. The education he had received as a child helped him understand issues clearly and use logic and reason to solve problems. By the time he was an adult, powerful men had learned to lower their voices and listen to what James Madison had to say.

James Madison's contributions to the United States went far beyond his accomplishments before and during the American Revolution. He helped create the Constitution, which remains the basis for the government of the United States of America. Later he served as the nation's fourth president.

Today James Madison is considered one of the greatest of America's "Founding Fathers." From his keen mind came vital and lasting contributions to a system of government that has served the United States so well for more than 200 years. Madison's mind, in turn, was shaped largely by the family beliefs instilled in him when he was a child and by the education he received while growing up.

A watercolor of the Madisons' magnificent home. James Madison grew up as the privileged oldest son of one of the wealthiest and most important families in Orange County, Virginia.

A Privileged Start

As a child, James Madison had some advantages that helped ensure his future success. He was born into a life of wealth, property, and power.

Almost 100 years before James Madison's birth, his great-great-grandfather had come to Virginia from England. His name was John Maddison, and he had been a ship carpenter. When he arrived in Virginia in 1653, Maddison was granted 600 acres of land in the colony.

John Maddison's estate, called Mantapike, was located on the Mattaponi River in Virginia. Over the next 30 years, he added to his lands. By the time of his death around 1683, the Maddison estate had grown to 1,900 acres along the York and Mattaponi Rivers.

Maddison's children continued to expand the family's holdings. They also intermarried with other wealthy families in Virginia. Around the year 1680 the spelling of the family name was changed to Madison.

James Madison's grandfather, Ambrose Madison, was one of the wealthiest men in Virginia. He owned a large *plantation* of more than 5,000 acres. When he died, most of this land was left to his young son, James.

James Madison Sr.—the father of President Madison—was just nine years old when his father died. While he was growing up, his mother ran the plantation. As James grew older, he started to take over more and more of the responsibility for running and managing the plantation. One of his first jobs was delivering tobacco to the warehouse of a man named Francis Conway, on the Rappahannock River, nine miles below Fredericksburg. One day, while making a delivery, he met Francis's daughter Nelly. The two fell in love, and in 1749, they married. James was 26, and Nelly was 17.

Their first child, James Madison Jr., was born on March 16, 1751, at Belle Grove, the plantation home of his maternal grandmother. Belle Grove was located in Port Conway, King George County, Virginia. Family letters that have survived say that young James—nicknamed Jemmy—was not a healthy baby. In fact, he suffered from poor health for much of his early life.

When Jemmy was born, his father was the wealthiest landowner in Orange County. As a prominent citizen, James Madison Sr. held many important jobs. He was a *magistrate* of Orange County and head of the county *militia*. He was also a leader in the local church.

The Madison family continued to grow. Nelly Madison gave birth to 11 more children after Jemmy. However, only Jemmy and six of his siblings survived to adulthood. As the oldest son, Jemmy would be *heir* to most of the Madison estate. This virtually guaranteed him a prosperous and secure life.

More than 100 slaves toiled in the fields of the Madison family's large plantation. As an adult, however, James Madison would be deeply troubled by the issue of slavery.

The family's prosperity was due in part to slavery. Slaves performed much of the labor on Virginia plantations. They cultivated and harvested the tobacco crops, and they performed many other tasks for their white masters. The Madison family owned more than 100 slaves.

The first slaves had been brought to Virginia in 1619. They were blacks who had been kidnapped from their homes in Africa by Portuguese men. The 19 slaves were chained and loaded onto a small ship, then taken across the Atlantic Ocean to be unloaded and sold in Jamestown, Virginia. Over the next

During James Madison's childhood, some Indian tribes allied themselves with the French and fought the American colonists. Years later, when Madison was president, the "peace medal" shown here was struck as a gesture of goodwill toward the Native Americans. The front depicts President Madison; the reverse, a handshake and a peace pipe over a tomahawk.

two centuries, more than half a million blacks were brought to America in much the same way. Slaves were usually permitted to marry other slaves, but at birth their children also became slaves.

Slavery helped the white landowners of Virginia become wealthy. A lot of work—much of it backbreaking—had to be done for a plantation to be profitable, and slaves were a source of cheap labor.

Life wasn't very pleasant for the slaves, however. They were considered property, and the plantation owner could sell them or order them to do whatever he wanted. When a slave owner died, his slaves were often sold to pay debts or given to his heir along with other possessions, such as a house, land, or livestock.

The issue of slavery would trouble James Madison later in his life. As an adult, he felt that slavery was wrong—

> James Madison owned about 100 slaves at the time of his death. He did not free them in his will because he felt doing so would sentence his wife, Dolley, to a life of poverty.

even though he continued to own slaves until his death. In the 1830s, when he was an old man, he became president of the American Colonial Society. This was an organization dedicated to taking freed slaves back to Africa. However, few freed slaves wanted to leave the United States. By that time nearly all of them had been born in America, and Africa was for them a strange and unknown land. Even some of James Madison's slaves begged him not to send them away. Documents from Madison's time show that he didn't mistreat his slaves. However, he didn't free them even after his death.

As a child, though, Jemmy didn't question slavery. To him, slaves were just part of life on the family plantation. It was only after years of education and experience that he began to have doubts about the practice of owning slaves.

A house slave fans the dinner guests on a southern plantation. James Madison's earliest education came simply by observing daily life at his family's Virginia estate. Later he was tutored at home by his mother and grandmother.

Growing up in Virginia

Jemmy Madison's earliest education came by following his father around the family estate. His parents wanted him to learn by observing nature firsthand. Jemmy was told to make the most of his senses: smelling, seeing, touching, tasting, and hearing almost every aspect of plantation life. Learning the basics of farming in Orange County, Virginia, would help make him a better farmer later in life.

As time passed, Jemmy's education moved indoors. His first teachers were his mother and grandmother. They taught Jemmy how to read, write, and solve simple math problems. Later, they taught him geography, history, and literature.

Jemmy had a sharp mind from a young age. However, his body was not as strong. Sometimes he became very sick. He occasionally suffered seizures, which may have been caused by a mild form of *epilepsy*. At times he also became sick with fever and with stomach problems.

But there were plenty of opportunities for fun during his childhood. Jemmy loved reading and playing games on the farm with his younger brothers, Ambrose and Francis. The three boys would sometimes get together with their cousins, who lived on nearby plantations. As they grew older, Jemmy and his brothers learned to ride horses and to care for the animals. These skills were necessary as well as fun, because horses were the fastest way to travel from place to place.

As Jemmy and his brothers grew up, they also learned to handle weapons, just like other youths living in Virginia and the American colonies during this time. Guns were used for hunting and, more important, for protection. The English colonists living in Virginia were fighting battles on the colony's western border against French settlers. The French had made *alliances* with Native American tribes, and the Indians also fought the English. The French and Indian War started in 1754, when Jemmy was about three years old. It would not end until 1763.

Jemmy's home was far from the fighting during the French and Indian War, however, so the Madisons and their Orange County neighbors went about their regular routines. One regular event that Jemmy probably enjoyed was "Court Day." Each month the leading property owners in Orange County would assemble in town. They served as judges, listening to legal cases and complaints. Many people who weren't involved in these legal matters would also come to town while the court was in session. When the court session ended, the people would celebrate together. Adults exchanged news and gossip, while children played in the streets. There was singing and other entertainment. Sometimes wrestling matches, three-legged races, and fiddle-playing competitions were organized.

Because Jemmy's father was a magistrate, he had to attend the monthly court sessions. Between his official duties and

A column of British soldiers on the march during the French and Indian War, which lasted from 1754 to 1763. The war never touched the Madisons directly, but later they, like the rest of the American colonists, would be asked by the British to shoulder the financial costs—a major factor leading to the American Revolution.

management of the plantation, James Madison Sr. had started work on a large new house, necessary because his family was growing so quickly. Finished in 1760, it was the first brick house built in the county. Slaves on the plantation had made the bricks. The glass windows had been brought from London.

When the new house was ready, nine-year-old Jemmy helped to move some of the lighter pieces of furniture into it. The large, elegant home was eventually given the name Montpelier. (The first recorded use of this name occurred in 1781, about 20 years after it was built.) James Madison would

When James Madison was nine, his family moved into Montpelier, a large, elegant structure that would serve as Madison's home for most of his life.

live in the house on the family plantation for most of his life.

When the Madisons moved into the house, Jemmy's brother Francis was seven years old and his brother Ambrose was four. Another sibling, Catlett, was two years old, but died soon after the family moved into the house. That same year, Jemmy's mother gave birth to his sister Nelly.

After the Madisons settled into the new house, they started to entertain, holding lavish parties for their friends and relatives. This was expected of wealthy families. As a result, there were frequently guests around the house. On occasion, more than 100 guests would come to a party. And because families had to travel—sometimes for many days—to visit the plantation, they would often stay for a week or more.

Those who stayed at Montpelier would have been struck by the spectacular view of the mountains. Jemmy loved Montpelier. Later in his life, he would say that the air there was clearer, purer, and healthier than anywhere else in the world.

But life at Montpelier was not without sorrows. Jemmy's maternal grandmother died when he was nine years old. Two years later his paternal grandmother died also. He had looked up to his grandmothers, and he felt their loss deeply.

The death of his paternal grandmother also marked the end of his education at home. James Madison Sr. had a library of 85 books—a large collection by the standards of the day. By the time Jemmy was 12 he had read every one of them. So for further education he was sent away from home to a boarding school. The school was located in King and Queen County, Virginia. An *immigrant* from Scotland named Donald Robertson taught the students.

Jemmy was homesick at first, but he soon enjoyed the adventure of being away from home. And he wasn't completely alone at the school. Five of his cousins were also enrolled.

Donald Robertson had graduated from the prestigious University of Edinburgh in Scotland. He taught the students mathe-

Although life for the Madisons at Montpelier was more comfortable than life in the 18th century for most other Americans, hardships still existed. There were epidemics of smallpox, malaria, and yellow fever—none of which had a cure. In 1761, smallpox spread through Virginia, but Montpelier escaped the epidemic.

matics, logic, philosophy, astronomy, geography, Latin, Greek, and literature. Jemmy also learned to speak Spanish and French—in a way. When he was attending college at Princeton a few years later, he was asked to be an *interpreter* for a visitor from France. Although he could understand most of what the Frenchman said, the visitor was completely unable to understand Jemmy's "French." Because of his teacher's heavy Scottish accent, Jemmy hadn't learned how to say the words correctly. He never did rid himself of the "Scottish French" Robertson had taught him.

But Jemmy thrived under Robertson's instruction. He studied books by the Roman writers Virgil, Horace, and Ovid, which he read in Latin. He also loved reading other books in Robertson's library: Aesop's *Fables*, Thomas à Kempis's *Imitation of Christ*, and Tobias Smollett's *History of England*. He read *The Spirit of Laws*, a book by the French political philosopher Charles de Montesquieu, which had a great influence on him and the other men who created the U.S. Constitution in 1787.

Another book Jemmy enjoyed was *The Spectator*, a collection of essays about life in England during the early 18th century. *The Spectator* inspired him greatly. "When I was at an age which will soon be yours," he wrote in 1829 to his 11-year-old nephew, "a book fell into my hands, which I read . . . with particular advantage. I have always thought it the best that had been written for cherishing in young minds a desire of improvement, a taste for learning, and a lively sense of the duties, the virtues, and the proprieties of life. The work I speak of is 'Spectator,' well known by that title. It had several

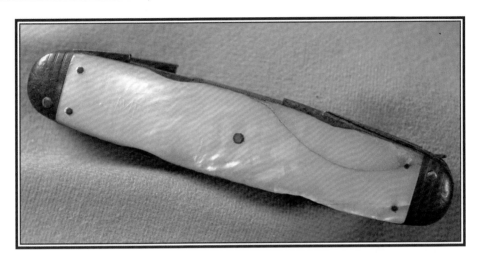

Two of James Madison's surviving possessions. Above: A pearl-handled pocketknife on which he etched the initial "M" (visible near the left). Most of the blades are broken, testifying to the frequent use to which he must have put the knife. At right: A small, handheld telescope called a spyglass, which—like nearly all the luxury items in the American colonies—would have been manufactured in Europe.

authors, at the head of them Mr. Addison. . . . Addison was of the first rank among the fine writers of the age, and has given a definition of what he showed himself an example. 'Fine writing,' he says, 'consists of sentiments that are natural without being obvious.' "

As a student at Robertson's school, Jemmy didn't just study the past. He also started learning about the political problems that were growing between England and the American colonies. By 1765, when Jemmy was 14 years old, the British government had imposed several new laws on the colonies. One of these was the Stamp Act, a tax on newspapers and other documents printed in the colonies. The money raised by this tax would help pay the cost of sending English troops to the colonies during the French and Indian War. Another new law was the Quartering Act. This required the colonies to pay the expenses when British troops were stationed in their territory.

Leaders in the colonies protested the Stamp Act, and it was soon repealed. However, during the next few years the British government would continue to force the colonists to pay taxes the Americans felt were unfair. This in turn would make many Americans angry at Great Britain.

Donald Robertson had a great influence on Jemmy. As a grown man, James Madison would say, "All I have been in my life I owe largely to that man." But in 1767, when Jemmy was 16, his father told him it was time to leave the school and return home. Jemmy was unhappy because he had hoped to continue his studies with Robertson. But James Madison Sr. had invited the new rector of the local church, the Reverend Thomas Martin, to live at Montpelier in

James Madison always recognized the value of education. When he died, he left his entire library to the University of Virginia and set aside $9,000 so that his nieces and nephews could go to school.

exchange for tutoring the Madison children. Martin had graduated from the College of New Jersey in 1762. (Today this
school is known as Princeton University.) One of his jobs at
Montpelier would be to prepare the Madison boys for college.

Once Jemmy and Martin got to know each other, they got
along well. During the next two years, they often discussed
history, politics, and religion.

One of the books Jemmy read around this time was *Letters
of a Farmer in Pennsylvania*. The author, John Dickinson, said
that Americans should protest British taxes. The colonies had
developed democratic assemblies, where representatives of
the people could decide issues that affected the colonies. Each
colony also had a governor, who was appointed by the king.
However, the governor had to respect the wishes of the colonial assembly. If he did not, the assembly could refuse to pay
his salary. But if the taxes were raised, Dickinson argued, the
British government could use that money to pay the colonial
governor's salary. The governor could then do what he
pleased, and it would mean the end of democratic government in America.

Jemmy read many other books and newspapers that
detailed the growing political problems between the government of Great Britain and the American colonies. He began to
experience strong feelings of *patriotism*. Like many other
Virginians, he began to identify himself as an American, not a
British citizen. These feelings of patriotism would grow as
Jemmy left home once again, this time to complete his education at college.

(Top) An early view of the College of New Jersey (today called Princeton University). James Madison arrived at the school in 1769 and, through hard work and determination, managed to graduate just two years later. (Right) Scottish-born John Witherspoon, named president of the College of New Jersey in 1768, was determined to make his school one of the best in the colonies. Dr. Witherspoon would later become a member of the Continental Congress and a signer of the Declaration of Independence.

Princeton

In 1769, James Madison was ready to start college. He needed to decide which school he would attend. There weren't many choices. Some young men from wealthy families sailed to England, where they could attend colleges like Oxford or Cambridge. Those who stayed in the colonies had a few major colleges to choose from. One was the College of William and Mary, which was located in Virginia near the capital of the colony, Williamsburg. The other schools were Harvard, located in Massachusetts; Yale, in Connecticut; and the College of New Jersey in Princeton, New Jersey.

Most boys from well-to-do Virginia families attended the College of William and Mary. However, James decided not to attend this school for several reasons. One of them was his health. He had always been a frail boy, and the area near the College of William and Mary was considered unhealthy. Also, around this time there was some tension at the college between the teachers and the administrators who ran the school.

James decided to attend the College of New Jersey in Princeton. It was closer to Virginia than either Harvard or

Yale—although it was still quite some distance away. But the influence of the Reverend Thomas Martin, his tutor, helped him make up his mind. Also, the year before, a prominent Scottish clergyman named Dr. John Witherspoon had been named president of the College of New Jersey. Bringing his hefty reputation to the young college, he set about making it one of the best in the colonies.

In the summer of 1769, 18-year-old James Madison set out from Montpelier. Thomas Martin went with him, as did the tutor's brother Alexander and a slave named Sawney. The trip to New Jersey covered more than 300 miles. Even with horses carrying the travelers and James's books and clothing, it took 10 hard days of travel to reach Princeton. A highlight of the trip for young James was the chance to see Philadelphia, which was the largest city in America at that time. After helping James settle in at Princeton, the Martins returned to Virginia with the slave Sawney.

Because James had such a good education already, he was able to skip some basic classes. This would help him finish college faster than other students.

Attending the College of New Jersey would prove to be a good decision. The college was the most *diverse* of the major colonial schools. Young men came from every colony to study in Princeton. When James entered the college, only 19 of the 84 students were from New Jersey. This

Among James Madison's classmates at the College of New Jersey were Aaron Burr, who would eventually become vice president of the United States, and Philip Freneau, later a well-known poet and publisher.

geographical diversity helped the students learn more about other areas of the colonies. After graduating, many of these students would return to their home colonies, where they would become teachers, judges, statesmen, and politicians. But they had learned how the issues of the day affected colonies other than their own. This would help as the idea of a united nation of states, rather than separate colonies, began to grow during the late 18th century.

James Madison's favorite subjects at college were history and government. His least favorite was public speaking. He lacked a strong voice and didn't like making speeches.

He was a dedicated student, studying late into the night. One of his friends, James Barbour, later said that young Madison slept only three hours a night because of all his studying. However, this tough schedule was hard on James physically, and he soon became sick. This forced him to spend less time on his studies in order to stay healthy.

> Although he was known as a good student, James Madison still liked to have fun. One of the pranks he and his friends played on other students while at the College of New Jersey was to put greasy feathers on the floor where classmates would slip on them. The friends also set off firecrackers in the rooms of new students.

Although students at the College of New Jersey had little time for themselves, James did find time to make friends and join in student pranks. He also did quite a bit of reading. Dr. John Witherspoon, the college's president, had added about 500 books to the school's library, and James tried to read as many as he could. He also continued to follow politics.

In the wake of the Boston Massacre—which occurred while James Madison was a student at the College of New Jersey—some Americans began thinking about a complete break with Great Britain.

James was inspired when he attended a protest bonfire at the college. He was horrified, however, when he heard what had happened to a group of citizens who had gathered to protest in Boston that year. The colonists' version of events—

the British would tell a somewhat different story—was as follows: A group of British soldiers had arrived and ordered the people in the crowd to go home. When the people refused, the soldiers fired into the crowd, killing five men. To the colonists, this became known as the Boston Massacre, and some soon began to talk openly about revolution. They felt it was necessary to break away from Great Britain's control.

After his first year at Princeton, James Madison decided he wanted to finish his education quickly. He and a friend named Joe Ross requested and were granted permission to take the courses of their last two years in one year. They worked hard, and James had to get by on just five hours of sleep a night. His courses during this year included Hebrew, religion, and ethics—studies that would have served him well if he had chosen to become a minister.

His devotion to his schoolwork allowed him to complete his degree in September 1771. But the hard work had taken a toll on his body. James was too tired and sick to attend the graduation ceremony. He was also not healthy enough to make the long journey back to Virginia, so he stayed at the school for about six months. He spent that time studying with Dr. Witherspoon.

In April 1772, James Madison's father wrote to him at the College of New Jersey. He asked his son to return to Virginia to teach his younger brothers. By the time James arrived at Montpelier, he was mentally exhausted. He couldn't seem to find enjoyment in life and was unsure about his future. James became even more depressed when he heard that his friend Joe Ross had died. He began to think he too might die young.

James Madison, fourth president of the United States, followed his friend, mentor, and fellow Virginian Thomas Jefferson into the White House in 1809.

President Madison

*I*t was politics that brought James Madison out of his funk. In 1773 the British government decided to allow a company to sell tea cheaply in the colonies. This would hurt the sales of American merchants. In Boston, a group of citizens dressed as Native Americans dumped a shipload of tea into the harbor. The British responded by passing a set of harsh new laws, which the colonists called the *"intolerable* acts," in 1774. There seemed to be no way to avoid war.

In 1774 James Madison became a member of the Orange County Committee of Safety. His job was to make sure people in the county were ready to fight if war broke out against England. He also became a colonel in the local militia.

In the spring of 1776, he represented Orange County at a meeting of Virginia's leaders at Williamsburg, the capital of the colony. On May 15, James and the other members of the convention voted for independence from Great Britain. Their vote told the Virginia *delegates* at the Continental Congress (a meeting of leaders from all over the colonies) in Philadelphia to prepare the Declaration of Independence.

As a member of the Virginia convention, James also helped

create a new state constitution. Because he hated public speaking, he didn't give passionate speeches during meetings, as men like Patrick Henry and Edmund Randolph did. However, he made his opinions known by speaking to members of the convention individually. Many of his views, especially with regard to religious freedom, were reflected in the final document.

From 1777 to 1779, James was involved in the state government at Williamsburg. He was a good writer, and Patrick Henry, Virginia's governor, gave him the important job of writing official state letters and papers. During this time James met another Virginian who would become a good friend and mentor: Thomas Jefferson. Although Jefferson was eight years older than Madison, they had many things in common.

In 1780, James was elected to the Continental Congress, which was acting as the national government during the American Revolution. He served in Congress for nearly four years. By the time he retired from Congress in 1783, he had earned a reputation as a well-informed and effective legislator. Despite his dislike of public speaking, he had even become an accomplished debater.

During this time the Revolution finally turned in favor of the Americans. In October 1781, a British general, Lord Charles Cornwallis, surrendered his army to George Washington. The American Revolution was over.

Winning the Revolution had been hard, because the British army was the best fighting force in the world at that time. However, the Americans soon found that creating a national government would be even harder. James Madison and others believed the goals of the Revolution could be fulfilled only under a strong national government. However, most Americans distrusted government because of the problems they had just been through with Great Britain. They didn't want to give a national government too much power.

The first government of the United States of America was set up under a document called the Articles of Confederation. It took effect in March 1781. However, there were many problems. The new government had no way to force the states to do things that were in the national interest. Also, the states refused to pay taxes to the national government, so the United States couldn't repay France and Spain the money those countries had loaned it to help fight the Revolution. Also, each of the states printed its own money, which led to other problems. One of these problems was an uprising of farmers in Massachusetts, called Shays's Rebellion, in 1786.

People realized that the weak national government set up under the Articles of Confederation wouldn't work. James Madison and others called for a convention in Philadelphia to write a new national constitution. The Constitutional Convention was held in 1787, with George Washington as its president. However, James Madison did much of the work of creating the Constitution. He proposed a plan that would give taxing and law-enforcement powers to the national government. James believed in a government that worked with a series of checks and balances. He supported a stronger *executive* branch, an independent federal *judiciary*, and a Congress with two chambers: the House of Representatives and the Senate.

When the delegates to the Constitutional Convention in Philadelphia signed the United States Constitution on September 17, 1787, that was only the first step in creating a new federal government. James Madison would play a key role in the next step: making sure the states ratified the document.

Because of his involvement and influence in creating the U.S. Constitution, James Madison has been nicknamed "the Father of the Constitution." He kept careful notes of the discussions and debates held during the Constitutional Convention. Those notes, published after he died, provide the only full record of what happened during the convention.

Writing the Constitution was only the first step, however. Only after 9 of the 13 states had voted to accept, or *ratify*, it would the Constitution become the law of the land.

The people who supported the Constitution called themselves Federalists. James Madison and two other leaders, Alexander Hamilton and John Jay, wrote a series of essays called *The Federalist Papers*. These were printed to convince people to vote for the new Constitution. James and the others did their work well. The Constitution was ratified by the summer of 1788 and became the law of the land. In April 1789, George Washington was elected the first president of the United States. James Madison was elected to the House of Representatives.

In 1794, when he was 43, James married a woman named Dolley Payne Todd. The couple settled in Philadelphia, which at the time was the nation's capital and which was, therefore, where Congress met. Though the Madisons would have no children together, James treated Dolley's son from her first marriage as his own child.

Dolley Payne Todd was a 26-year-old widow when she married Congressman James Madison, 43, in 1794. As first lady, she would be known for her skills as a hostess and for saving White House papers and valuables—including a famous Gilbert Stuart portrait of George Washington—from advancing British soldiers.

During the presidency of James Madison, long-standing tensions with Great Britain finally erupted into the War of 1812. Here British troops burn the White House, 1814. President Madison and his advisers had evacuated the capital in advance of the redcoats.

James retired from Congress in 1797. He and Dolley returned to Virginia, where he worked on his plantation and added to the family house. He also worked hard to make sure Thomas Jefferson—his friend and neighbor in Virginia—was elected president in 1800. When Jefferson was successful in his presidential bid, he named James Madison secretary of state in 1801. With Jefferson and Secretary of the Treasury Albert Gallatin, James helped influence policy and politics. Among his important work as secretary of state was guiding the negotiations for the Louisiana Purchase in 1803. This was an agreement to buy a huge area of land west of the Mississippi River from France. The purchase doubled the territory of the

United States, adding nearly a million square miles.

In 1808, at the end of Jefferson's two terms, James Madison was elected president. But he inherited some problems that had arisen with other countries. Eventually, the United States would again become involved in a war with Great Britain.

The War of 1812 did not go well for the United States. By 1814, British troops were in North America, fighting to a standstill on the Niagara frontier and moving into the Chesapeake Bay, with the intent of taking Washington. A small but powerful British unit won several important battles, eventually burning the Capitol and the White House.

Despite this *demoralizing* defeat, the Americans held off a British attack on Baltimore. This battle inspired Francis Scott Key to write "The Star-Spangled Banner." By Christmas Eve of 1814, a peace treaty was signed. It restored the prewar boundaries and ensured continued independence for America.

James Madison left the presidency in 1817 and returned to Montpelier with Dolley. As he embarked on the farming life, Dolley helped him prepare his papers for eventual publication. In 1829, James served as a delegate to Virginia's second constitutional convention. He was the only member who had attended the first convention. This marked his last appearance in public. As time passed, he grew weaker and spent more and more time at Montpelier.

James Madison Jr. died on June 28, 1836, at his family home. He was 85. But his legacy lives on in many ways—most importantly in the U.S. Constitution, which more than 200 years later remains the basis of government in the United States.

CHRONOLOGY

1751   James Madison Jr. born on March 16 at Port Conway, King George County, Virginia.

1761   Moves with his family to a new home, known as Montpelier.

1762   Attends a plantation boarding school run by
–67   Donald Robertson.

1769   Attends the College of New Jersey (now Princeton
–71   University).

1776   Elected delegate to the Virginia Convention and the General Assembly.

1787   As one of Virginia's delegates to the Constitutional Convention,
–88   plays a major role in creating the U.S. Constitution; with John Jay and Alexander Hamilton, writes *The Federalist Papers* in support of ratification of the Constitution.

1789   Elected to the House of Representatives; sponsors the Bill of Rights; works with Thomas Jefferson to form the Democratic-Republican Party.

1794   Marries Dolley Payne Todd on September 15.

1801   Appointed Thomas Jefferson's secretary of state; holds position until 1809.

1808   Elected fourth president of the United States.

1812   Reelected as president; War of 1812 begins.

1814   British troops burn Washington; peace treaty with British signed in December.

1817   Retires to Montpelier; with help from wife, Dolley, begins preparing his papers for future publication.

1829   Serves as delegate to Virginia's second constitutional convention.

1836   Dies June 28 at Montpelier.

GLOSSARY

alliance—an association of two groups or nations who agree to cooperate to achieve a common goal.

boycott—to refuse to deal with a person or organization as a protest against that person or organization.

delegate—a person who is chosen to represent a larger group of people at a meeting or conference.

demoralizing—discouraging or dispiriting; having the effect of eroding or destroying the confidence of a person or group.

diverse—made up of different types, such as people from different places or with different backgrounds.

epilepsy—a medical disorder characterized by loss of consciousness and sudden convulsions.

executive—the branch of a country's government responsible for enforcing the laws.

heir—a person who receives, or inherits, family property after the death of a parent or parents.

immigrant—somebody who moves to a country intending to settle there.

interpreter—somebody who translates what is said in one language into another language, so that speakers of different languages can communicate.

intolerable—so unpleasant or painful that it cannot be endured.

judiciary—the branch of a country's government that oversees the courts and dispenses justice.

magistrate—a judge with authority over local matters and minor crimes.

militia—a group of civilians who take military training so that they can serve as an army during emergencies.

Parliament—a law-making assembly, made up in part of representatives elected by the people, in nations such as Great Britain.

patriotism—pride in or devotion to one's country.

plantation—a large estate or farm, especially one in the American South before the Civil War where crops such as tobacco and cotton were tended by resident slave laborers.

ratify—to give formal approval to something, usually an agreement negotiated by somebody else, so that it can become valid.

repeal—to officially revoke or abolish a law.

FURTHER READING

Clinton, Susan. *James Madison: Fourth President of the United States.* Chicago: Childrens Press, 1986.

Fritz, Jean. *The Great Little Madison.* New York: G. P. Putnam's Sons, 1989.

Malone, Mary. *James Madison.* Springfield, N.J.: Enslow Publishers, 1997.

Marcovitz, Hal. *The Constitution.* Philadelphia: Mason Crest Publishers, 2003.

Morris, Richard B. *Witness at the Creation: Hamilton, Madison, Jay, and the Constitution.* New York: Holt, Rinehart and Winston, 1985.

Peterson, Merrill D., ed. *James Madison: A Biography in His Own Words,* Volume 1 and 2. New York: Newsweek Books, 1974.

Pflueger, Lynda. *Dolley Madison: Courageous First Lady.* Springfield, N.J.: Enslow Publishers, 1999.

INTERNET RESOURCES

- http://www.jmu.edu
  Website for James Madison University.

- http://www.whitehouse.gov/history/presidents/jm4.html
  White House website for former presidents.

- http://www.leftjustified.com/leftjust/lib/sc/ht/fed/mbio.html
  Website that examines the roots of constitutional government in the United States and around the world.

- http://www.jamesmadisonmuseum.org
  Museum dedicated to the memory of the fourth president of the United States.

- http://www.law.emory.edu/FEDERAL/federalist
  Website dealing with *The Federalist Papers*, authored by Alexander Hamilton, John Jay, and James Madison.

INDEX

PICTURE CREDITS

3: Bettmann/Corbis
8: North Wind Picture Archives
12: Réunion des Musées Nationaux/Art Resource, NY
15: Courtesy of the Colonial Williamsburg Foundation
16: Special Collections, Carrier Library/James Madison University, Harrisonburg, VA
18: North Wind Picture Archives
21: North Wind Picture Archives
22: Carl & Ann Purcell/Corbis

25: Special Collections, Carrier Library/James Madison University, Harrisonburg, Virginia
28: Princeton University Library; Independence National Historical Park
32: Burstein Collection/Corbis
34: Réunion des Musées Nationaux/Art Resource, NY
38: Art Resource, NY
39: Hulton/Archive/Getty Images
40: North Wind Picture Archives

Cover photos: (left) National Archives; (center and right) Independence National Historical Park, Philadelphia

Contributors

ARTHUR M. SCHLESINGER JR. holds the Albert Schweitzer Chair in the Humanities at the Graduate Center of the City University of New York. He is the author of more than a dozen books, including *The Age of Jackson*; *The Vital Center*; *The Age of Roosevelt* (3 vols.); *A Thousand Days: John F. Kennedy in the White House*; *Robert Kennedy and His Times*; *The Cycles of American History*; and *The Imperial Presidency*. Professor Schlesinger served as  Special Assistant to President Kennedy (1961–63). His numerous awards include the Pulitzer Prize for History; the Pulitzer Prize for Biography; two National Book Awards; the Bancroft Prize; and the American Academy of Arts and Letters Gold Medal for History.

LISA KOZLESKI is a newspaper reporter at *The Morning Call* in Allentown, Pennsylvania, and has lived in and worked for newspapers in Colorado, Washington, Philadelphia, and England. In 1995 she moved to the Philadelphia area, where she lives with her husband, John Harding, and their dog Kaia. This is her third book for young readers.